For my mother, who encouraged me to dream. —T. T.

For the dreamers of the world. —J.S.G.

The GIRL Who Buried Her DREAMS in a CAN

by Dr. Tererai Trent ❧ illustrated by Jan Spivey Gilchrist

VIKING

An Imprint of Penguin Group (USA)

SHE WAS *SUPPOSED* TO BE A BOY. Her parents even chose a respectful Shona name fitting a boy—*Tereraishokoramwari*, meaning "listen to the word of the spirit."

But on this cold winter morning in a small village in what is now Zimbabwe, *she* emerged—a ball of fire as brilliant as the sunrise.

The baby's grandmother quickly snipped the birth cord and wrapped it tightly inside a piece of cloth torn from the mother's dress. Then she buried the cord deep beneath the red earth.

"This is our ancient way," the grandmother said. "The child whose birth cord is buried in the ground will always remember her home."

The little girl grew up in a hut, its roof thatched with grass and its walls made of mud.

Each day, she tended to the family's cattle and fetched water and firewood from many miles away. Sometimes she ran into older boys carrying books on their way to school. Oh, how she longed to trade her firewood for books!

But for most little girls in her village, learning and school were *hatigone*—"impossible." If families had any money for school, they sent boys. Girls were needed at home to cook, clean, and bring supplies.

Every woman in the little girl's family had heard the word *hatigone*. It was never more painful than when the little girl watched her aunt's dark eyes fill with tears because she couldn't read a letter from her husband. She had no choice but to ask a stranger to read it aloud.

"This shouldn't be!" the little girl shouted to her mother and grandmother.

The women agreed.

"We need a young woman to be our eyes, to read and write for us," her grandmother said. "Maybe it will be you, dear child."

The little girl decided she would be their eyes. She would learn to read and write!

She borrowed her brother's schoolbook and flipped through the crisp pages. It was filled with pictures of smiling people, big cities, and tall buildings.

Her brother, Tinashe, called the book by a funny name—geography. My, my, my, how the word tickled her tongue!

"I will teach you how to read and write," he said. "But you must keep it a secret. And you must do something for me in return."

The little girl grinned and made a promise.

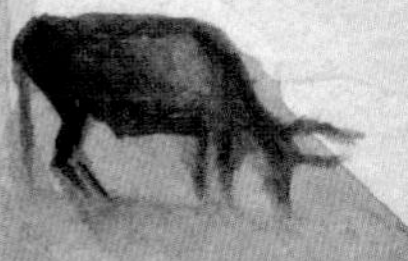

Tinashe taught the little girl how to read the Shona way, through song. She learned the vowels and consonants, tracing each letter in her brother's workbook as she sang their sounds.

Just as she'd learned how to sew cloth to make a quilt, the little girl learned to sew vowels and consonants together to make words. Oh, how the letters held secrets in the way they formed words. And the words held secrets in the way they told stories!

Sometimes she focused so intently on her lessons, she'd forget to watch the cattle, leaving them to stray and graze in neighboring maize fields.

The little girl learned quickly. Soon she could read *baba* and *amai*, the Shona words for mother and father.

And she learned to complete Tinashe's homework, her payment for the reading lessons.

When Tinashe's teacher discovered the siblings' secret, he begged the little girl's father to let her attend school.

But before the little girl could enroll, she was asked to perform a test, as every child must. She stretched each arm around her head, one at a time, to touch the end of her earlobes. If she could reach, she was ready.

Oh, how happy she was when she felt the tips of her earlobes with her fingers!

The little girl loved learning so much that she couldn't bear to stop when the school day was over. The maize fields became her classroom, and the cattle became her students. She gave her students names and taught them science and math—her favorite subjects.

As she solved math problems with her grazing cattle, the other village children pointed and stared.

"Why does she bother to talk to animals?" they'd say. "They can't learn!"

Soon after the little girl started school, her village began to change.

War and drought pushed the men of the village into the factories of the city and the gold mines near the mountains. When they returned, they rested under the broad leaves of the *muchakacha* trees. They hung battery-operated radios from branches, enjoying news of the world.

As the little girl did her homework, she'd listen, too. The radio programs took her to faraway places. Australia! Europe! America! She wondered if she'd ever see them.

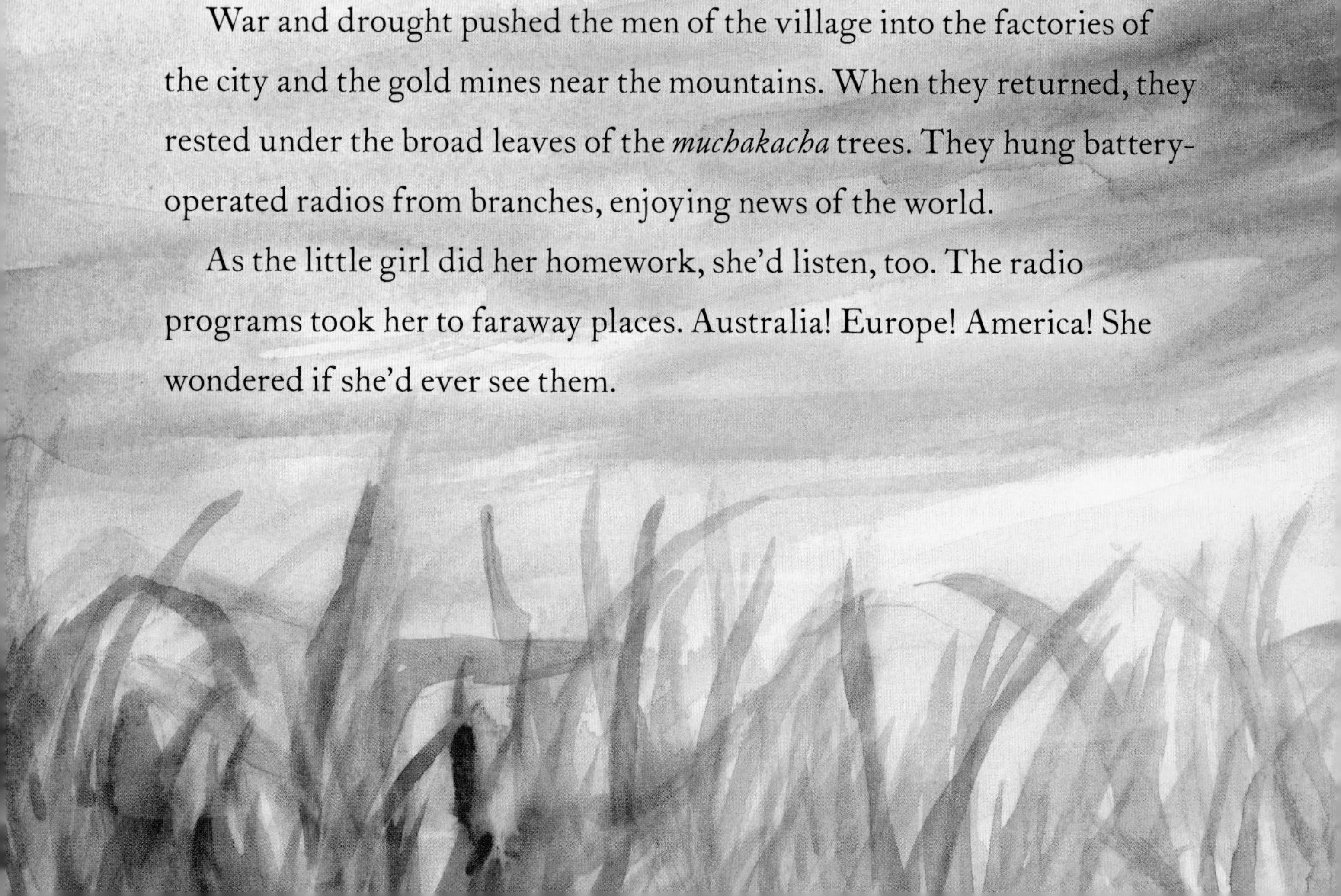

Geography

Moons rose and set, and the little girl became a young woman, a wife and mother. Her village became something new as well. The end of war brought hope and change for the next generation of boys and girls.

The young mother's heart grew each time she sent her children to school. She fed and loved them as she fed and loved her dream of learning.

Others fed her dream, too. Zimbabwe welcomed strangers from faraway lands—educated men and women who had come to learn more about the young mother's village and share stories of other countries.

One story stole the young mother's heart. In America, both men and women could study their favorite subjects for as long as they wanted.

Before she knew it, her dream had grown. An education . . . but in America!

A kind visitor named Jo Luck took the young woman's hand. "If you truly desire this dream," she said, "then it is achievable."

"Achievable?" the young woman repeated. "*Tinogona!*" she whispered in Shona.

What a powerful word for a dreamer.

The young woman ran to tell her mother.

"You must write down your dreams and bury them beneath the ground," her mother said. "Mother Earth will feed them and help them grow."

It was an ancient ritual, like the burying of the birth cord.

"Trust the universe, daughter, to honor your dreams."

The young woman quickly scribbled four dreams on a scrap of paper: to travel to America; to earn one degree; then a second, even higher; then a third, the highest.

She placed the paper in a worn tin can.

"Wait!" her mother called. "Your dreams will have little meaning, daughter, unless they bring gifts you can return to your people. Always remember your home."

So she added a fifth dream: to give education back to her village. Then she buried her can in the field where she had once watched cattle graze.

"*Tinogona!*" she sang.

It was a special day when the young woman received a letter with a strange stamp and a university seal at the top. After years of studying and hard work, she was finally going to America!

But before she could pack her bags, the young woman needed more money for travel. How would she get it?

The young woman's mother visited the headman of the village. He had great respect for the young woman and her buried dreams.

Without her knowledge, the headman asked each villager to give whatever they could to make the young woman's journey possible. Some sold their chickens, mangoes, and groundnuts to help her. Others gave pennies as a symbol of their love and support. Her dreams were coming true!

When the young woman boarded the plane to America, she thought of her mother. When she started her first day of school, she imagined her brother's face. When she found herself at the university library late at night, she remembered her village. When she struggled to put food on the table for her children, she recalled Jo Luck's words. And whenever she felt her dream slipping away, she whispered, "*Tinogona.*"

Tinogona
geography

It *was* achievable.

The young woman earned one degree; then a second, even higher; then a third, the highest.

And finally, her last dream was fulfilled. She brought education to the little girls and boys of Zimbabwe, as she had promised many moons ago.

Dear Reader,

AS A YOUNG CHILD growing up in rural Rhodesia (now known as Zimbabwe), my life was shaped by poverty, back-breaking labor, and the horrors of raging war. But school and books showed me another world—a magical place where malnutrition and violence were not part of daily reality. I wanted that life—a life where I had access to an education, plenty to eat, and peace. My mother and grandmother made me believe that I had the power to change my life and even the world. And later, Jo Luck—an aid worker from America—taught me a word that set me on my path: achievable.

Tsvangirayi Mukwazhi

I am a firm believer that education is the way out of poverty. And I know the opportunities I've been given mean little if I do not share them. In July of 2011, my foundation broke ground on a project to rebuild my childhood school, Matau Primary School. With the generous help of Oprah Winfrey, Save the Children, and others, Matau is now equipped with brand-new classrooms, a playground, a library, and a borehole providing clean water. My foundation brings educational resources to nearly five thousand children in Matau and throughout the neighboring communities across the region. And not only do girls attend classes, but they do so confidently and in greater numbers.

Eileen Burke

Teachers, parents, relatives, and friends can play a crucial role in the development of our greatest resource: our children. It is my hope that this story will inspire children to dream and work hard. And it is also my hope that it will encourage those involved in children's lives to remind them that their dreams are achievable.

Tererai

Tsvangirayi Mukwazhi

AFTERWORD

DR. TERERAI TRENT graduated with a bachelor's and master's in plant pathology from Oklahoma State University; a master's in public health from UC Berkeley; and a PhD in evaluation from Western Michigan University. Since graduating, she has also been awarded four honorary degrees. She founded the Tinogona Foundation in 2011—now called Tererai Trent International (TTI)—to improve the lives of children in rural Africa. When she isn't teaching as an adjunct professor at Drexel University and leading projects with TTI, Dr. Trent speaks all over the world on the topics of education and women's rights.

Western Michigan University

VIKING
Penguin Young Readers Group
An imprint of Penguin Random House LLC
375 Hudson Street
New York, New York 10014

First published in the United States of America by Viking, an imprint of Penguin Random House LLC, 2015

LIBRARY OF CONGRESS CATALOGING-IN-PUBLICATION DATA IS AVAILABLE.

ISBN: 978-0-670-01654-9

1 3 5 7 9 10 8 6 4 2

Manufactured in China   Set in Caslon Twelve